EXPLORING SCIENCE

SHIPS & BOATS

SAIL • NAVIGATION • RADAR • ANCHOR • KEEL

**With 17 easy-to-do experiments
and 300 exciting pictures**

CHRIS OXLADE
CONSULTANT: TREVOR BLAKELEY

ARMADILLO

This edition is published by Armadillo, an imprint of Anness Publishing Ltd, 108 Great Russell Street, London WC1B 3NA; info@anness.com

www.annesspublishing.com

If you like the images in this book and would like to investigate using them for publishing, promotions or advertising, please visit our website www.practicalpictures.com for more information.

PICTURE CREDITS
b = bottom, t = top, c = central, l = left, r = right
Ancient Art and Architecture Collection/M Andrews: page 9bl. Barnaby's Picture Library: pages 8b, 22t, 63c; /D Coutts: page 57tr. Corbis: page 57cl. Mary Evans Picture Library: pages 8t, 13c&br, 15t&cl, 44t. FLPA/Celtic Picture Library: page 57tl; /S Jonasson: page 34cr; /P & A Lewis: page 53c; /R Tidman: page 34t. Robert Harding Picture Library/ A Woolfitt: page 19cr. Michael Holford: pages 9c&br, 10t, 12t, 16t, 24t. Garmin: page 53tcr. Hulton Getty Picture Collection: page 14b. Hydrotère/Francoise Robert: page 39b. Image Select: page 28t; /C.F.C.L: pages 8c, 16c&b, 19cl, 34cl, 42b, 52br, 53cl&cr, 62t; /Ann Ronan: pages 14t&c, 57b. iStock: pages 33c, 59b. Kos Picture Source Ltd: pages 5tl, 12bl, 19t, 23tl, 25t, 29b, 38c&b, 45t, 49cl, 51cl; /C Borlenghi: pages 5c, 25cl, 63br; / H Gunn: page 48c; /R Jewell: page 48t; /G Norman: page 25cr; /G M Raget: page 53br; /F Taccola: page 56c; /D Williams: pages 29t; 53bl. /Crown Copyright: page 44br, 59cl; /R Adshead: page 43tl; /P Russel: pages 42t, 43tr,cl&b. Jenn Lang: page 48b. National Maritime Museum Picture Library: pages 4b, 13t&bl. P&O Cruises: pages 17tl,c&b, 49cr. Planet Earth Pictures: pages 5b, 9t, 18c, 45br, 51b; /R de la Harpe 35cr; /N Wu: page 45bl. QE Class Carriers: page 43cr. RNLI: page 59tl; /R Tomlinson: pages 58b, 59tr. PlanetSolar: page 23bl. Science Photo Library/S Fraser: page 56b; /D Nunuk: page 29cl. Seaco Picture Library: pages 17tr, 28b, 32c. Stena Mediabank: pages 32b, 33t. Stock Market: pages 4t, 5tr, 22b, 23tr, 29cr, 30t, 33b, 35cl, 39tr, 49tr, 50t&b, 51t, 58t&c, 62b; /M K Daly: pages 18b, 49tl; /R Soto: page 36t; /T Stewart: page 35t. TRH Pictures: pages 44bl. Trip: page 62c; / T Bognar: page 12br; /G Hopkinson: page 22c; /D Houghton: page 51cr; /H Rogers: pages 24b, 63t; / R Surman: page 56t; /B Turner: pages 28c, 63bl. Yamaha: page 23br. US Navy/William Jamieson: page 42c. www.f1boatphotos.com: page 49b&64b.

Publisher: Joanna Lorenz
Editors: Sue Grabham, Charlotte Hurdman, Elizabeth Young
Photographer: John Freeman
Designer: Caroline Grimshaw
Picture Researcher: Annabel Ossel
Illustrator: Peter Bull Art Studio
Production Controller: Pirong Wang

Manufacturer: Anness Publishing Ltd, 108 Great Russell Street, London WC1B 3NA, England
For Product Tracking go to: www.annesspublishing.com/tracking
Batch: 7196-22993-1127

We would like to thank the following children, and their parents, for appearing in this book: Mohammed Afsar, Anthony Bainbridge, Amaru Fleary, Ricky Garrett, Africa George, Francesca Hill, Carl Keating, Mai Peterson, Susy Quirke, Kirsty Wells.

CONTENTS

WHAT IS A SHIP?

PEOPLE HAVE used rafts, boats and ships to travel across water for many thousands of years. At its simplest, a ship is any craft that travels on water, but ships have developed from simple log rafts to vast oil tankers. This development has affected life on land, in shipbuilding yards and at ports where hundreds of people work loading and unloading cargo. The difference between a ship and a boat is not very clear. Generally, ships are larger and travel across seas and oceans. Boats are smaller and usually travel on rivers, lakes and coastal waters. Ships and boats come in a huge variety of shapes and sizes and have a wide range of uses from simple rowing boats to massive cruise liners. The selection of ships and boats shown here illustrates the wide range of jobs they do, and their importance for transport, commerce, leisure, exploration and combat. Simple projects will help you understand the technical side of ships – how they float and how they are powered and controlled.

Boats on inland waters
Two types of boat common on rivers and canals are shown here. In the foreground is a very simple rowing boat. It has many uses – transport, fishing and ferrying from ship to shore. It is usually propelled by oars, but it can be fitted with sails or an outboard motor. Behind is a narrow, flat-bottomed canal boat. It is used for transporting cargo.

Parts of a ship
This fishing trawler looks similar to many other ships and boats. The body of the boat is called the hull. The backbone of the hull is the keel. The bow (front) is sharply pointed to cut easily through the water. A deck provides a watertight covering for the crew to work on. An engine-driven propeller pushes the ship along. The rudder at the stern (back) is used for steering.

deck   mainmast   bridge   funnel   mizzen mast (back mast)   lifeboat   stern

bow   hull   keel   propeller   rudder

Fishing boats

One of the earliest uses of boats was fishing. Today there are fishing boats designed to catch different fish in all sorts of conditions – from calm lakes to the deep oceans. Fishing trawlers drag nets through the water behind them.

Cargo carriers

The largest moving machines ever built are big cargo ships. There are several types designed to carry different types of cargoes. The one pictured here is a container ship, which carries different cargoes packed in large metal boxes.

Fast and fun

The fastest boats are racing powerboats. They are just one of many different types of boats used for having fun on the water. Their hulls are designed to rise out of the water and skim the surface at high speed. The deep V-shape of the hull helps the bow to lift clear of the water and slice through the waves.

Under the water

Submersibles and submarines are the only types of boat designed to travel under the water as well as on top. The submersible shown here is just breaking the surface of the water. Submersibles are small craft used for underwater research, exploration and repairs to seabed pipes and cables. Submarines are usually larger and most are for military purposes. They are used to launch missiles and sink ships. Most submersibles can dive much deeper than a military submarine.

HOW DO SHIPS FLOAT?

S HIPS AND all other objects that float can do so because the water they are floating in pushes upwards against them. This pushing force is called upthrust. An object will float if the upthrust of the water is great enough to overcome the downwards push of the object's weight. The size of the upthrust depends on how much water the object pushes out of the way. When you put an object in water and let it go, it settles into the water, pushing liquid out of the way. The farther it goes in, the more water it pushes away and the more upthrust acts on it. When the upthrust becomes the same as the object's weight, the object floats. If, when the object is fully underwater, its weight is bigger than the upthrust, however, it will sink. The simplest boats, such as rafts, float because the material they are made of is less dense (lighter) than water. Heavy metal ships float, because they are specially designed to displace (push aside) a large weight of water. Not all water has the same density. Salt water is denser than fresh water and gives a stronger upthrust. Ships float higher in salty seawater than in fresh lake water.

fresh water   *salt water*

Measuring density
The density of water is measured with a hydrometer. Make a simple hydrometer by putting non-hardening clay on the end of a straw. Put it in a glass of water. Mark the water level with tape. Put the straw in an equal amount of salty water. What happens?

TESTING UPTHRUST

You will need: *two polystyrene (styrofoam) blocks (one twice the size of the other), wooden block, marble.*

1 Put the two polystyrene blocks into a tank of water. They will float well, because their material, polystyrene, is so light. Only a small amount of upthrust is needed.

2 Push the blocks under water. Now you are pushing lots of water aside. Can you feel upthrust pushing back? The bigger block will experience more upthrust.

3 A wooden block floats deeper in the water, because wood is more dense (heavier) than polystyrene. A marble sinks, because the upthrust on it is not as great as its weight.

HOLLOW HULLS

You will need: *scissors, kitchen foil, ruler, marbles.*

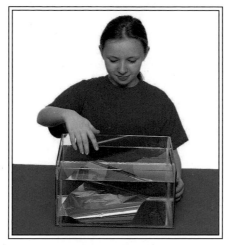

1 Put a piece of foil 20 x 15cm/ 8 x 6in into a tank of water. With only a slight push, it will sink. This is because it does not displace much water so there is little upthrust.

2 Lift the sheet of foil out of the water. Now form it into a simple boat shape with your fingers. Take care not to tear the foil.

3 Put your foil boat back into the tank of water. It should now float. Its shape pushes aside much more water than it did when it was flat, so the upthrust is greater.

4 Try filling your foil boat with small objects such as marbles, for cargo. As you put more marbles in it will float lower and lower. How many marbles can your boat hold before it sinks?

the boat shape traps air inside it and pushes aside more water

Foil float

This simple foil boat works like a real ship's hull. Even though it is made of metal, it is filled with air. This gives the hull shape a much lower overall density.

THE FIRST BOATS

NOBODY KNOWS exactly when people first started using craft to travel on water, but it must have been tens of thousands of years ago. The first craft were probably extremely simple – perhaps just a log, an inflated animal skin, or a bundle of reeds tied together. People discovered that craft like these, made from what was available close by, could help them to cross a stretch of water more easily. These craft probably developed into early simple boats, such as dug-out canoes and skin-covered boats, in which a person could sit while fishing or moving along a river. The basic designs are still in use in many areas of the world today and have many advantages over modern boats. They are simple to make from cheap local materials. Although they are not very long-lasting, there are no high-tech materials to mend or engine parts to replace. The simplest boats do not use up expensive fuel or hard-to-find equipment such as batteries.

Simple raft
A raft like this one from Australia can be built with very basic tools. It is used in shallow water and propelled along with a long stick pushed into the riverbed. Rafts are probably the oldest form of water transport. Aboriginals may have used sea-going rafts to first reach Australia around 55,000 years ago.

FACT BOX
• In 1970, Norwegian Thor Heyerdahl built a large Egyptian-style reed boat called *Ra II*. He sailed it from Africa to the Caribbean. This proved that the Egyptians would have been able to reach America more than 4,000 years ago.

• One of the greatest sea battles of all time took place at Salamis, off Greece, in 480BC. In the battle, 380 Greek triremes defeated an invading fleet of around 1,000 Persian ships.

Dug-out canoe
A dug-out canoe is made by hollowing out a thick tree trunk to leave a thin wooden hull. The hull is smoothed and shaped so that it moves easily through the water. Dug-out canoes are fairly heavy boats and sit low in the water.

Yak-skin boat
This strange-looking boat was photographed on a river in Tibet, now part of China. It is made by stretching yak hides (a type of ox skin) over a wooden framework. The hide is then treated to make it waterproof.

Inuit kayak

The kayak was developed by the Inuit people of the Arctic. It is also a hide boat, made from sealskin stretched over a driftwood frame. Kayaks were used as fast hunting craft for harpooning seals, fish and walruses. Boats like this work well in rough seas. A skilled paddler can turn the kayak upright if it capsizes (rolls over).

Nile boat

A model boat from an ancient Egyptian tomb shows the type of craft used on the river Nile about 5,000 years ago. Boats like these were the first to use a simple sail. The boat was propelled with oars when there was no wind or the wind was in the wrong direction. It was steered using a long oar hanging over the stern.

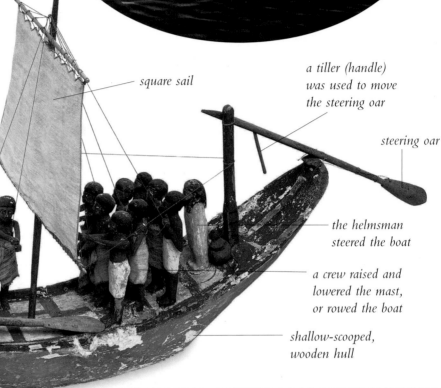

square sail

a tiller (handle) was used to move the steering oar

steering oar

rigging (ropes and poles)

the helmsman steered the boat

a crew raised and lowered the mast, or rowed the boat

shallow-scooped, wooden hull

oar

passenger

Greek warship

This is a full-scale replica of an ancient Greek trireme. A trireme was a warship with three banks of oars operated by about 170 men. Triremes attacked other ships by ramming them. Soldiers were also transported on deck.

Roman galley

A Roman mosaic from Tunisia, made around AD200, shows that Roman warships were very similar to earlier Greek ships. In the stern they often had wooden towers painted to look like stone. Underneath the high bow was a ram.

MAKE SIMPLE BOATS

YOU CAN build your own models of ancient types of boat that are still in use today. Instructions for making a model reed boat are given in the first project. Reed boats are made by tying thousands of river reeds together into huge bundles. The bundles themselves are then tied together to make hull shapes. Small reed boats are still built in southern Iraq and on Lake Titicaca in South America. In ancient Egypt, quite large boats were made like this from papyrus reeds. Some historians believe that Egyptians may have made long ocean crossings in papyrus craft. The model in the second project is of a craft called a coracle. This is a round boat made by covering a light wooden frame with animal hides. Like reed boats, coracles are still made, but today builders use a covering of canvas treated with tar instead of hide. They were small enough for one person to paddle along a river and were used for fishing. Look for pictures of other simple craft and try making working models of them, too.

Chariots, boats and bladders
A stone carving from 860BC shows Assyrian soldiers crossing the river Tigris. They are transporting a war chariot in their coracle-like boat. Assyrian soldiers also used inflated pig's bladders as buoyancy aids to help them swim across wide rivers.

MAKE A REED CRAFT

You will need: large bunch of raffia, scissors, ruler.

1 Make bundles of raffia by tying a few dozen strands together with a short length of raffia. Make two bundles about 20cm/8in long and two more about 25cm/10in long.

2 Tie the two long bundles and the two short bundles together. Tie the short bundles on top of the long ones. Fix a strand between each end to make the ends bend up.

3 Gently lower the reed boat on to the surface of a tank of water. How well does it float? Does it stay upright? Try leaving it in the water to see if it becomes waterlogged.

MAKE A CORACLE

You will need: *scissors, craft cane, string, dark cotton cloth, PVA/white glue, paint brush.*

1 Cut one long and three short pieces of cane. Using short lengths of string, tie all three short pieces to the long piece to make a triple-armed cross.

2 Cut a much longer piece of cane. Form it into a loop and tie it to all the ends of the triple cross shape. Bend the ends of the cross up as you tie them to form a dish shape.

— *waterproof covering*

lightweight frame

Model of an ancient craft
The design of the coracle has not changed in thousands of years. Early Britons used them 9,000 years ago. They are light to carry, easy to manoeuvre and stable enough to fish from.

3 Cut pieces of cotton cloth about 15x5cm/6x2in. Apply glue to the outside of the frame and put the pieces over it. Glue the pieces to each other where they overlap.

4 Glue down the cloth where it folds over the top of the frame. Put two coats of glue on the outside of the cloth to waterproof it. Leave the glue to dry completely.

5 When dry, put the finished coracle into a tank of water. How well does it float? Why not try making a person from modelling clay to sit in your model coracle?

THE AGE OF SAIL

S AILS CAPTURE the wind and use it to push ships and boats along. As far as experts can tell, sails first appeared on ships on the river Nile in about 3500BC. These ships had just one simple square sail on a single mast. They were only useful when the wind was blowing in the same direction as the crew of the ship wanted to go. If the wind was blowing in another direction, such as from their destination, the crew had to row there instead. Viking boats in the AD600s used square sails to sail the coasts of Scandinavia. Later, large coastal Viking ships crossed the Atlantic to reach North America. In the Middle Ages, the lateen (triangular) sail was invented by the Chinese and Arabs. The lateen sail allowed ships to be sailed with the wind from the side. From the 1100s, European sailors began building fully-rigged ships with a combination of square and lateen sails. This allowed them to make the maximum use of the wind. Their boats also had sturdy, seaworthy hulls. In ships like these, European sailors began long voyages of exploration.

Viking sails

A stone carving from Sweden that dates from the AD700s shows a Viking merchant boat with a simple square sail. The sail was made from cloth reinforced with diagonal strips of leather. Sails like this helped the crew sail downwind.

Chinese way ahead

The Chinese developed multi-masted ships called junks. These used triangular sails several centuries before they were introduced to Europe. This modern junk has sails that hang from poles that are hauled up the mast. The sails can swivel around the mast to take advantage of wind from behind or the side. They are made with cloth stiffened by bamboo poles. The poles keep the sails flat, make it easy to fold up the sails and provide a handy ladder for the crew.

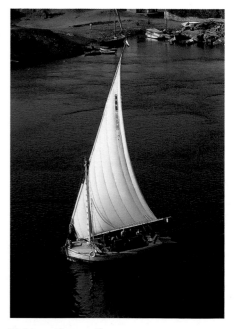

Triangular sails

This fishing boat on the river Nile is called a felucca. Its design has been in use for 1,000 years and is most often seen on Arab trading vessels called dhows. The single triangular sail is an example of a lateen sail.

A mixture of sails

This painting shows ships off the coast of Portugal in the 1520s. The large ships are heavily-armed carracks, a design that used both square and triangular sails. Smaller carracks were used as merchant vessels. The flagship *Santa Maria*, which took Columbus to America in 1492, was probably a small carrack.

Men-of-war

These French ships are typical of the men-of-war (warships) that developed by 1700. They had many rows of cannons and hulls that were richly carved and gilded.

Life onboard

A cartoon shows sailors celebrating victory in battle with Admiral Nelson in 1798. Hundreds of men were needed to sail a man-of-war. They lived in cramped conditions on the gun decks. Tables and hammocks were suspended between the guns.

The golden age of sail

By the 1850s, sleek, fast and efficient ships called clippers carried cargo such as tea and wool around the world. They represented the peak of sailing ship design and were the largest wooden vessels ever built. Larger merchant ships with iron hulls and up to seven masts were built up to the 1930s.

STEAM POWER

Stoking the boilers
To create steam, stokers constantly fed the fire boxes under a ship's boilers with coal. It was hot, unpleasant work in the stokehole.

T HE FIRST steam engines were developed in the early 1700s for pumping water out of mines. By the end of the century they had become small and more efficient and engineers began to use them in trains and ships. Steam power meant that a ship could keep going even if the wind was in the wrong direction, or not blowing at all. The first craft to use steam power was a small river boat called the *Charlotte Dundas*, launched in 1802. At sea, steamships carried sails to save fuel when the wind was blowing in the right direction. Early steamships used paddles, but propellers gradually proved to be more efficient. After the 1850s, shipbuilders began to use iron instead of wood. The superior strength of iron meant that much larger ships could be built, which could also be fitted with more powerful steam engines.

Crossing the Atlantic
The huge *Great Eastern* was built in 1858. Steamships arrived at a time when crossing the Atlantic Ocean was becoming more popular. Steam power allowed faster and more reliable crossings, which people were willing to pay for. The *Great Eastern* could carry 4,000 passengers. It was the only ship to have both paddles and a propeller. But passengers did not quite trust steam, so it was also fitted with sails.

An iron monster
This print shows the construction of the *Great Eastern's* central compartment. At 210m/689 ft long and 32,000 tonnes, it was by far the largest ship in the world at its launch in 1858. It was the last of three revolutionary ships designed by British engineer Isambard Kingdom Brunel. The *Great Eastern's* design was copied on other steamships for several decades. The hull was divided into ten watertight compartments, with double iron plating from the keel to the waterline. It took three months and seven attempts finally to launch the *Great Eastern*. Unfortunately, it had a pronounced and unpleasant roll in heavy seas. It was sold for scrap in 1888.

Paddle-powered riverboats on the Mississippi

On the shallow rivers of the southern United States, steam powered riverboats with huge paddles were developed. Here, two riverboats are racing each other on the Mississippi River in about 1850. Riverboats had flat, shallow hulls and no keel. Paddlewheels were mounted on each side, or at the stern.

Steaming to war

Steam power and iron construction gave warships much greater speed, manoeuvrability and strength. *Dreadnought,* built in 1906, was the fastest battleship of its day and became the model for the period.

Tramp steamer

A typical cargo ship was known as a three-island steamer. This was because it had three raised decks, or islands. They were also called tramp steamers if they sailed from port to port with no fixed route.

Luxury travel

As transatlantic travel grew, shipping companies built large, luxurious ships called liners. This 1920s poster is from the golden age of the liner. Rival companies competed to provide the quickest crossing.

poop deck (third island)

mainmast

a funnel carries smoke and steam from engines away from the deck

central island

foremast

cargo boom

fo'c'sle or forecastle deck (first island)

SHIPBUILDING

Viking boatbuilders
This is part of the Bayeux Tapestry. It shows Norman shipwrights building the fleet that invaded England in 1066. The Normans were descended from the Vikings and shared many of the same boatbuilding techniques. They used special tools, such as axes and augers (hole borers), to shape the hull of a ship. Slender, Viking war boats were called longships.

S HIPS ARE constructed in a shipbuilding yard. Large ships are usually made from steel. Generally, the hull is built first by welding pieces of steel together. Often the hull is built in large sections that are then welded together. When the hull is finished, the ship is launched on to the water, where the rest of the ship is completed. Dozens of different tradespeople, such as welders, crane drivers, painters, electricians and carpenters work in shipyards. Boatbuilding takes place in smaller boatyards. Boats are usually made from wood or glass-reinforced plastic (GRP).

Shipbuilding methods have changed as new materials have become available. Originally all ships were made from wood. A skeleton hull was made, then covered with planks. Steel ships are built with the metal skin forming part of the structure. New ships are designed on computer and models of them are tested before being built.

Wooden ribs
Here, the ribs of a wooden boat are being attached to the central keel. The timbers form a skeleton frame to which the planks of the hull and deck will be attached.

FACT BOX
• The size of a ship is given in gross registered tonnage (g.r.t.). This is not a measure of its weight, but of the space inside it. One ton equals 2.8 cubic metres/100 cubic feet.

• The displacement of a ship is equal to the weight of the water that it pushes out of the way when it floats. This is usually equal to the weight of the ship and everything on it.

• The deadweight of a ship is the difference between the ship's displacement when empty and when it is full. It measures the weight of the cargo and passengers.

Covering the hull
Planks are attached edge to edge to the ribs of a wooden boat to make a smooth hull. The tight-fitting planks will be given several coats of paint or varnish to make a completely watertight finish.

Naval architects

Just as there are architects who design buildings, there are naval architects who design ships. These architects are planning the deck layouts of a cruise liner.

Shipbuilding shed

This picture shows the bow section of the superferry *Stena Britannica* under construction. You can see the steel decks, bulkheads (watertight walls and doors) and skin. The ship is being built in a huge construction shed, where its progress is unaffected by the weather.

Float out

Once the hull has been completed, the floor of the construction shed is flooded so that the entire hull can be floated out. Here, the cruise liner *Oriana* is being floated out at its launch. Smaller ships are built on slipways and then launched by sliding them down into the water.

Fitting out

Work on electrical equipment, lighting, pipes and other fixtures and fittings is completed after the ship is launched. This process is called fitting out. After fitting out, the ship will undergo sea trials.

HULLS

THE MAIN part of a ship is the hull, which sits in the water. The hull does four things. It provides the strong, rigid shape that makes the structure of the ship. It is a waterproof skin that stops water getting in. It supports all the equipment in the ship, such as the engines, and it provides space for the cargo. The shape of the hull also lets the ship slide easily through the water. The hull shape of a ship or boat depends on what that ship or boat is designed to do. Long, thin hulls are designed for moving at speed, while broad hulls are designed to carry as much cargo as possible. Wide, shallow hulls float high in the water and are good for use on shallow lakes, rivers and canals. The hull shape also dictates the stability of the ship, or how easily it tips from side to side. Inside the hull, solid walls called bulkheads make the hull stiffer and divide it into a number of watertight compartments.

Hulls for floating
Try pushing a light ball underwater. It will spring back up. Upthrust from the water makes a hollow hull float in the same way.

Multi-hulls
This canoe will not tip over because it has outriggers. The outriggers work like small hulls on each side of the canoe, making it a very stable vessel. Catamarans (boats with two hulls) and trimarans (three hulls) work in the same way. Boats with only one hull are called mono-hulls.

Plastic hulls
A white-water kayak has a one-piece hull made of tough, rigid plastic. Its materials are strong enough to resist bumping against rocks and the riverbed. The hull's long, thin shape is designed for speed, slicing through the rough water. The canoeist sits in a sealed cockpit, which prevents water getting in. This not only keeps the canoeist dry, but means that the kayak remains buoyant (afloat).

Hulls in halves

Here, two halves of a yacht hull are made from GRP (glass-reinforced plastic). GRP is made by filling moulds with layers of glass fibre and glue. It is light but strong and has a smooth finish.

Points and bulbs

While a fishing boat is in dry dock it enables us to see the parts of the hull usually underwater. The bulb shape at the bottom of the bow helps the boat to slip more easily through the water.

Changing shape

If you could cut through a ship and look at the cut ends, you would see a cross-section of its hull. Here you can see how the cross-section of a container ship's hull changes along its length.

Overlapping planks

This is a head-on view of the bow of a 1,000-year-old Viking ship. The hull is made from a shell of overlapping planks, hammered together with nails and strengthened by internal ribs. Hulls constructed of overlapping planks are called clinker built.

stempost

ocean-going high bow

wide, stable hull shape

16 overlapping oak planks

keel

Stern cross-section
The sides curve inwards to make the bottom narrower than the deck.

Central cross-section
The hull is almost square. This allows the maximum space for cargo.

Bow cross-section
Just behind the sharp bow the bottom is very narrow and the sides are high.

FAST AND SLOW

WHENEVER AN object such as a ship moves through the water, the water tries to slow it down. The push that the water makes against the object is called water resistance, or drag. The faster the object moves, the bigger the water resistance gets. If you look around a busy harbour, you will see dozens of different hull designs. Sleek, narrow hulls with sharp bows cause less resistance than wide hulls with square bows, so they can move through the water faster. You can test how the shape of a bow affects the speed of a ship in the project below. The deeper a hull sits in the water, the more resistance there is. Some hulls are designed just to touch the water. For example, a small speedboat has a flaring, V-shaped hull designed to skim across the surface. A cargo ship, however, has a more square-shaped hull that sits lower in the water. Speed is not so important for the cargo ship as it is for the speedboat. Instead, the cargo ship is designed for stability and to carry the maximum amount of cargo.

TESTING HULL SHAPES

You will need: *stiff card (card stock), pen, ruler, scissors, sticky tape, kitchen foil, paper clips, non-hardening clay, scales, string, watering can, plastic tub three wooden bricks.*

Templates
Use these three templates to help you cut out and make the three boat shapes in this project. Their dimensions are about 15cm/6in long, by 10cm/4in wide. Make the sides of each boat shape 3cm/1¼ deep.

1 Use a ruler to carefully draw out the three templates shown above on sheets of stiff card. Make sure the corners are square and the edges straight. Cut out the shapes.

2 Using scissors, score along the lines inside the base of each shape (shown as broken lines above). Bend up the sides and use sticky tape to fix the corners together.

3 Make the round-ended and pointed boats in the same way as the first boat. Use a separate piece of card to make the round bow and tape to the base in several places.

4 Now cover the outside of each shape with foil, neatly folding the foil over the sides. This will make the shapes more waterproof. Fix a paper clip to the bow of each boat.

5 Roll out three balls of clay to the size of a walnut. Weigh the balls to make sure they are the same weight. Attach a ball to the bow of each boat with string.

6 Put a large plastic tub on to a table or a strong box. Fill the tub with water to about 1cm/½in from the top of the tub.

Try timing the boats with a stopwatch. You could find the difference between the fastest and slowest boats.

8 Release the boats all at the same time. The weighted strings will pull them along down the length of the trough. Which one wins the race to the other end of the trough?

7 Line up the boats at one end of the tub. Hang the strings and clay balls down over the other end of the trough. Put a wooden brick inside each boat.

The shapes on test
Boats' hulls are usually pointed to help them cut through the water. Energy is wasted pushing a flat end through the water, which makes a boat slower.

SHIP POWER

Punting

In a punt, a person stands on the back of the boat to push down on a long pole against the bottom of the river. Each push propels the boat forwards. The pole is also used to steer the punt and keep it straight.

THERE ARE many different ways of propelling boats and ships through the water. The most basic, such as rowing and paddling, are human-powered. Oars and paddles work by pushing against the water. Today, they are only used in small vessels. Sails harness the natural power of the wind to propel a boat or ship. Engines convert the energy stored in fuel into the movement of a propeller. As the propeller spins, its blades force water to rush backwards, which thrusts the boat or ship forwards. Most engines used in boats and ships are diesel engines. Other types of marine engine are petrol (gasoline), gas turbine and steam turbine engines. Some short-distance ferries move by pulling themselves along a wire or chain attached to the bank on the other side of a lake or river. Other craft, such as hovercraft, have aircraft-like propellers. These are useful in very shallow or plant-filled water where an underwater propeller could be easily damaged.

FACT BOX
• In 1845, a ship with a propeller easily won a tug-of-war with a ship with paddlewheels.

• In the future, boats may lift up out of the water altogether. Wingships use air pressure to skim above the water's surface. They can fly along about 2m/6½ft above the waves.

• In the swamps of Louisiana, people travel in swamp skimmers pushed along by a huge fan at the back.

Rowing with oars

An oar is a long pole with a flattened blade at one end. It is fixed to a pivot on the edge of the rowboat, called a rowlock. The rower sits backwards and propels the boat forwards with a continuous cycle of strokes. Rowing a boat using a pair of oars is called sculling.

Paddles

A dragon boat from Hong Kong is propelled along by a team of paddlers. A paddle is a short pole with a flat blade at one end used to propel a canoe. Paddles are easier to manoeuvre than oars, but they are not so efficient.

Propeller power

A propeller is made up of several angled blades (usually between two and six) attached to a central hub. The enormous propeller being checked here will be one of a pair used on a large cruise liner. Its blades are specially curved to cut down turbulence as water is drawn past the hull. Each propeller will be driven by an electric motor.

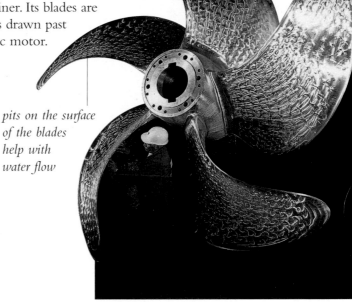

pits on the surface of the blades help with water flow

Capturing the wind

Sails catch the wind and push a boat along. The sailors adjust the position of their sails to make the best use of the wind. These yachts have the wind blowing from behind and are using large sails called spinnakers for extra speed.

housing for petrol (gasoline) engine

throttle (controls speed)

clamp

driveshaft

propeller

Portable power

An outboard motor is a self-contained portable power unit for small boats. It is attached to the stern of the boat by a strong clamp. A petrol (gasoline) engine at the top drives the propeller via a driveshaft. Twisting the throttle controls the speed of the propeller. Moving it from side to side changes the direction of the boat. When not in use, the whole engine can be unclamped.

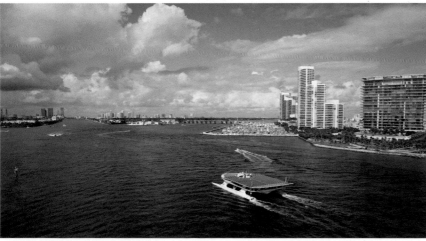

Solar power

In May 2010, the *Tûranor PlanetSolar* was the first solar-powered boat to travel around the world. It is topped with 500 sq m/5,382 sq ft of solar panels. Sunlight is converted to electricity by solar cells and temporarily stored in batteries, which are used to power the electric motor.

CONTROLLING A SHIP

A LL SHIPS and boats have simple controls for steering. Usually this is a rudder at the stern. The rudder is controlled by a tiller (handle) or wheel. The rudder only works when the boat or ship is moving through the water. Powered craft also have engine controls for adjusting speed. Many boats have twin propellers and can also be steered by running the engines at different speeds or in different directions (forwards or reverse). Large ships may also have bow and stern thrusters, which are used in port to push the ship sideways or rotate it on the spot. On modern cruise liners, which often have to enter a different dock every night of the cruise, the ship can be moved by means of a small joystick on the bridge. Large modern ships have a computerized autopilot like that on an aircraft. This automatically adjusts the rudder and engine speed to follow a set course.

Simple rudder

The rudder on a Norman ship from the Bayeux Tapestry is a single oar. The long oar is set on the right side of the ship at the stern. Many early boats were steered with simple side rudders like this.

flow of water   *boat goes straight*

flow of water is deflected left

boat turns to the left

boat travels ahead

rudder

rudder is turned to left

rudder straight

How a rudder works

The rudder works by cutting into the flow of water. With the rudder in the middle, water flows past each side and the boat goes in a straight line.

When the rudder is turned to the side, the flow of water is deflected away to that side.

The water pushes against the blade of the rudder. This makes the stern go to the right, swinging the bow left.

When enough turn has been made, the rudder is brought back to the middle. The boat straightens out and travels ahead on its new course.

Under the stern

Here, the propeller and rudder of a cargo ship are being cleaned of barnacles in dry dock. In almost all ships and boats, the rudder is fixed behind the propeller under the stern. The rudder is turned by machinery in the stern that is controlled from the bridge. The propeller pushes water past the rudder, which makes the ship easier to turn from side to side at slow speed.

mainsheet

tiller
extension

tiller

rudder

Tiller control

In small boats, such as this sailboat, the rudder is turned from side to side by hand using a handle called a tiller. Here, the helmsman is using an extra handle, called a tiller extension. This allows him to lean out farther from the side of the boat to counteract the push of the wind against the sail. The sailors control the sails by means of ropes called sheets.

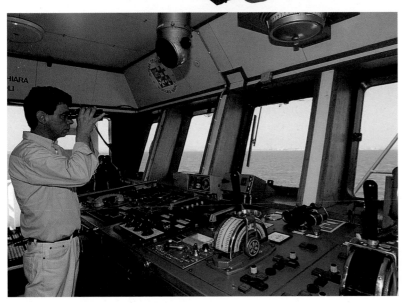

On the bridge

The bridge (also sometimes called the wheelhouse) is the control point of a ship. There are rudder and engine controls and navigation equipment, such as a compass and radar. The bridge is high up on the ship to give good, all-round visibility.

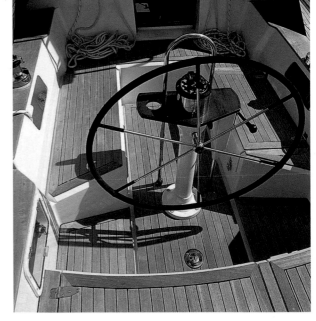

Steering wheel

On larger yachts a tiller would be too cumbersome to use. Instead, the rudder is operated by a large wheel linked to the rudder by a system of pulleys. The helmsman steers the yacht from the cockpit.

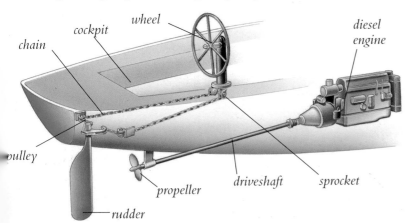

chain

cockpit

wheel

diesel
engine

pulley

propeller

driveshaft

sprocket

rudder

Connecting up the wheel and the propeller

In this large cruise yacht, the rudder is moved by wires linked to the wheel in the cockpit. The wheel drives a sprocket, which moves a chain. Wires attached to the chain move the rudder via a set of pulleys. The yacht is also equipped with a diesel engine that is connected to a single propeller via a driveshaft. A soundproof engine room insulates the hull from noise and vibration made by the engine.

POWER AND STEERING

THE PROJECT below will show you how to build a simple boat driven by a propeller and controlled by a rudder. The propeller is powered by the energy stored in a wound-up rubber band. The two blades of the propeller are set at different angles and push the water backwards as the propeller spins. In turn, this makes the boat move forwards. When you have built your model, you could try making other designs of propeller (for example more blades set at different angles) and testing them to see which works best. After making the propeller you can add a rudder. The rudder can be moved to different positions to make your model boat turn to the left or right, but it will work only when the boat is moving along. Without the rudder, the boat does not go in a straight line very well. So, as well as making the boat turn from side to side, the rudder also helps your model (as it does a full-size boat) travel straight ahead.

Simple propeller
The simplest propeller has two blades that twist in opposite directions. This is the propeller of a small pleasure boat. Three- and four-bladed propellers are more powerful. The hole in the middle is where the driveshaft from the engine fits into the propeller.

MAKE A POWERED BOAT

You will need: *cork, bradawl (awl), scissors, small plastic bottle, large plastic bottle, large paper clip, ruler, pliers, bead, long rubber bands, small pencil, thin garden cane.*

1 Make a hole through the middle of the cork using a bradawl. Cut a diagonal slot in either side of the cork. Push two strips of plastic cut from a small bottle into the slots.

2 Cut an oblong strip from one side of the large plastic bottle. This slot is the top of your boat. With the bradawl, make a small hole at the back of your bottle in the bottom.

3 Straighten a large paper clip with pliers. Bend the last 1.5cm/½in of wire at right angles. Push the wire through the cork and thread it through the bead and small hole.

4 Bend over the end of the wire inside the bottle. Hook a rubber band over the wire and stretch it up through the neck of the bottle. Secure in place with a pencil.

the model will go in circles

5 To wind up the band, turn the pencil as you hold on to the propeller. Keep holding the propeller until you put the boat into the water and release it. What happens?

6 Now make a rudder for your boat. Cut a piece of plastic about 4x4cm/1½x1½in and pierce two holes near one edge. Push thin cane through the two holes.

Straight and turning
This is the finished model of the boat. To test the controls, start with the rudder centred to make the boat go straight. How tight a circle can you make your boat turn in?

rubber band engine

propeller

rudder

8 Fix the rudder support to the bottle with a rubber band so that the rudder is clear of the propeller. Wind up the rubber band and put your boat back in the water. Try turning the rudder from side to side. What happens?

7 Use the strip of plastic cut from the large bottle to support your rudder. Pierce two holes about 2cm/¾in apart in the centre of the strip and push the cane through.

CARGO SHIPS

CARRYING CARGO has always been the main job of ships. Even today, in the age of air travel, it is still the cheapest way of transporting goods. In fact, more that 95 per cent of goods are transported around the world in the holds of cargo ships. A cargo ship is basically a long, box-shaped vessel, providing the maximum amount of room inside for cargo. The first cargo ships carried their cargoes in barrels or jars in the hold. Modern ships have been developed to carry specific cargoes, such as oil and cars. There are still many general cargo ships, including container ships. Different types of cargo ship have also been developed for use in rivers, in coastal waters and for long-distance ocean travel. Ocean-going ships are huge and expensive to build, so they are designed to spend as little time as possible in port.

Canal-sized
The Panama Canal in Central America provides an important short-cut for ships travelling between the Atlantic and Pacific oceans. Many cargo ships are built to dimensions called panamax – the largest size that can fit through the canal.

Parts of a container ship
A container is a standard-sized, steel box that can be filled with any sort of cargo. On a container ship, the prepacked containers are stacked in piles in the hold and on the deck. Some of the containers on deck may be refrigerated. The ship is driven by a giant diesel engine.

River barge
A slow, wide barge carries cargo along the river Rhine in Germany. The river reaches from the North Sea deep into the industrial heartland of Germany. Coal, grain and timber are often carried by barges like this one.

hydraulically operated container crane

containers stacked on deck using cell guides

bridge

crew's quarters

bow thruster

single main propeller

Unloading containers

In port, giant cranes transfer the containers from the ship. The standard-size containers are lowered on to specialized trucks, which carry them to huge dock-side parking lots where they are stacked in rows. The containers are then loaded on to trucks or railway (railroad) cars and taken to their final destination.

FACT BOX

• The longest ship ever built was *Mont*, which was 458m/ 1,503ft long. It operated under various names between 1979 and 2010, including *Knock Nevis, Jahre Viking* and *Seawise Giant*.

• The largest container ships in the world are the Triple E class vessels, at 400m/643km long. A Triple E class ship can carry up to 18,000 6m/19ft long containers.

Return to sail

A few cargo ships have experimental computer-controlled sails. The rigid sails are used to save fuel. When set, they move automatically. They are rotated by electric motors guided by computer. Sails like this are very efficient at achieving the best angle to the wind.

Not too deep

Load lines (also called Plimsoll lines) show how low a ship is safely allowed to float in the water when it is fully loaded. The load lines on the left of the picture are for different types of water. TF means tropical fresh, F is fresh water, T is tropical salt water, S is salt water in summer and W is salt water in winter. The scale on the right shows the distance to the keel of the ship in metres.

Specialist carriers

This ship is specially designed to carry just one sort of cargo – liquefied petroleum gas (LPG), such as methane or butane. The gas must be cooled to a very low temperature to keep it liquid. The pipes on the deck control the gas.

SHIP STABILITY

Many ships look top heavy, so how do they manage to stay upright and not capsize? These projects will help you find out what makes a ship stable. The shape of the hull's cross-section is important – some hull shapes are more stable than others. When a ship tips over, the hull on that side sinks into the water. On the other side it rises up out of the water. The water creates more upthrust on the side that sinks in, pushing the ship upright again. The more one side of the hull sinks in, the bigger the push and the more stable the hull. The position of the cargo in the hull is important, too. Heavy cargo high up on deck makes the ship top heavy and more likely to tip over. Heavy cargo or equipment low down in the hull makes the ship more stable. Cargo that can move is dangerous, because it could slip to one side of the ship, making it more likely that the ship will tip over. The first project looks at the stability of a multi-hulled boat called a catamaran.

Pile it high
Containers are piled high on the deck of a container ship. The containers are loaded evenly to prevent the ship from becoming unstable.

Two hulls
The two hulls of a catamaran are joined together by a strong bridge. This double-hulled shape makes the boat very stable.

MAKE A CATAMARAN

You will need: *small plastic bottle, scissors, thin garden cane, rubber bands, some small wooden blocks or other cargo.*

1 Remove the top from a small plastic bottle and carefully cut the bottle in half lengthways. This will leave you with two identical shapes to form the catamaran hulls.

2 Place the two halves of the bottle side by side. Lay two medium-length pieces of garden cane on top. Securely fasten the canes to the bottle halves using rubber bands.

3 Put your completed catamaran into a tank or bowl of water. Load the hulls with cargo such as wooden blocks. Can you make your boat capsize?

LOADING CARGO

You will need: *plastic bottle and square tub of about the same size, scissors, wooden blocks, non-hardening clay.*

1 For this project you need one container with a round hull shape and another about the same size with a square hull shape. Cut a strip from the round container to make a hold.

2 Put both containers in a tank or bowl of water. Gradually load one side of each hull with wooden blocks. Which hull capsizes first? Which hull is more stable?

3 Load the square hull evenly with wooden blocks. You should be able to get a lot more in. Press down on one side of the hull. Can you feel the hull trying to right itself?

Unstable round hull
When a round hull tips to one side, there is little change to the amount of hull underwater. This makes the shape unstable.

Stable square hull
When a square hull tips to one side, there is a great change in the amount of hull underwater on that side. This makes it stable.

4 To stabilize the round hull, press some lumps of clay into the bottom of the rounded hull. This adds weight called ballast to the bottom of the hull.

5 Reload the round hull with wooden blocks. Can you see how the ballast low down in the hull has made the craft more stable?

FERRIES

Cable-drawn ferry
This ferry travels along a chain stretched between the two river banks. Its engine pulls on the chain instead of working a propeller.

FERRIES ARE ships and boats designed to carry passengers, cars, coaches, trucks and sometimes even trains across water. There are several different types of ferry. Each one is designed for a different type of crossing, such as small, raft-like ferries for short river crossings of a few minutes, or larger cruise-liner ferries for long sea crossings of several days. Most vehicle-carrying ferries have wide doors and ramps at the bow and stern. These allow cars and lorries to drive quickly on and off the ship. They are known as a roll-on, roll-off (or ro-ro) ferry. In a typical large ferry, the lower decks are like a multi-storey car park. The passengers travel on the upper decks, where there are lounges, restaurants and stores. Ferries like this work day and night, all year round. Some ferries, such as catamarans, hydrofoils and hovercraft, are designed for short sea and lake crossings and are much faster.

FACT BOX

• The largest superferries can carry 230 cars, 30 trucks and more than 1,300 passengers.

• Train ferries carry railway (railroad) coaches (cars) and wagons. They have tracks on deck that the coaches roll on to at the docks.

• The world's fastest ferry is called the *Luciano Federico*, with a top speed of 111.5kph/69mph. It operates between Uruguay and Argentina.

Loading and unloading
Cars drive along a ramp to reach the car deck of a small ro-ro ferry. The ferry's bow slots into a special dock for loading. The ferry will be unloaded through stern doors. Larger ferries have separate ramps for loading cars and lorries (trucks).

Superferry
The huge ferries that travel on long sea routes are called superferries. They can carry hundreds of cars and lorries and thousands of passengers. There are cabins for passengers to sleep in on overnight sailings and stores, restaurants and cinemas to keep people entertained.

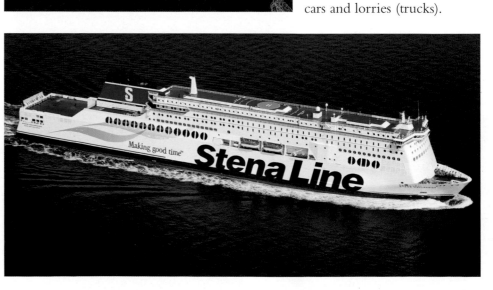

Speedy cat

Catamarans like the *Stena Explorer* are some of the fastest vehicle-carrying ferries in the world. *Stena Explorer* is powered by four gas turbines, which make this ferry much faster than a traditional passenger ferry.

Flying in water

A hydrofoil is the fastest type of ferry. Under its hull there are wing-like foils. These lift the hull clear of the water as it speeds along. Lifting the hull out of the water reduces water resistance (drag), allowing the hydrofoil to travel much faster.

lift

curved upper surface

flow of water

flat lower surface

low speed

high speed

How a hydrofoil works

Water flows faster over the foil's curved upper surface than it does over the flat lower surface, so creating lift. Foils only work when travelling at high speed. At low speed the boat's hull sits in the water.

How a hovercraft works

A central fan draws in air and forces it between the hull and the skirt. Two large pusher propellers drive the craft along.

pusher propeller   *flow of air*   *central fan*

buoyancy tank   *air cushion*

Hovering on air

A hovercraft skims across water supported on a cushion of air. The air is held in place by a rubber skirt. A hovercraft can also travel on flat ground, so it can leave the water to load and unload. Buoyancy tanks stop the hovercraft sinking if the air cushion fails.

FISHING BOATS

THERE ARE millions of fishing boats in the world. Most of them are small traditional boats sailed by a single person or a small crew. Others are larger, commercial fishing boats. The very largest, called factory ships, are able to stay at sea for up to a month. Fishing was one of the earliest uses of boats and dozens of different styles of fishing boat have been developed all over the world. Some fish are caught with hooks and lines or traps, such as pots (crates), left in the sea and attached to the seabed by an anchor. Most fishing, however, is done with nets that trap shoals of fish. Different types of net are used to catch different species of fish. Commercial fishing boats have special equipment for handling the nets and storing the fish they have caught. Many also have sonar equipment for tracking shoals of fish. In the 1970s many countries' fishing industries collapsed through over-fishing. International regulations now limit the number and size of fish caught in order to preserve fish stocks.

Fishing fleets
Coastal towns and villages all over the world have their own fishing fleets based in small harbours. This one is on the island of Skye in Scotland. Most people in the town are involved in the fishing industry. Laws to reduce catches and conserve fish stocks have hit many small ports.

Inshore fishing boat
This is a typical wooden fishing boat used for fishing in inshore (coastal) waters. It is used up to 100km/60 miles from port and catches surface-living fish such as herring, and mackerel.

Deep-sea trawler
Ships designed for fishing hundreds of kilometres off shore have high bows for breaking through waves. Trawlers like this catch fish such as cod and hake.

drift nets can be 100km/60 miles long and 60m/197ft deep

The mesh of a long drift net traps fish swimming close to the surface. They are slowly dragged through the water by boats called drifters. Drift nets catch many other sorts of marine life, not just fish, and are banned by many countries.

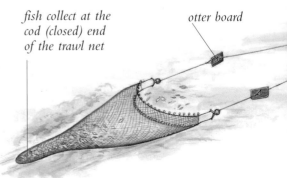

fish collect at the cod (closed) end of the trawl net

otter board

Bringing in the catch

A net bursting with cod and other fish is hauled on board. Fishing nets are pulled in after they have been in the sea for a few hours. A mechanical hoist lifts the full net out of the water. The net's closed end is released and its catch emptied out on deck.

Processing the catch

A catch is sorted as soon as it is on board. The fish may be cleaned and gutted before being frozen. Larger trawlers have equipment on board to process the fish – cutting off heads and tails and removing the bones.

A dip net is used to scoop up fish over the side of the boat.

Traditional fishing

Off the coast of Tanzania, East Africa, many fishermen use outrigger sailboats and dhows. Small fishing boats like these have not changed for many centuries. Nets, lines and spears are used to bring in the catch. Small-scale fishing like this does not deplete fish stocks as large commercial vessels can.

dip net

floats keep the top of the net on the surface

A shoal near the surface of the sea is quickly encircled by a purse seine net. The net is closed by gathering together the bottom edges like a purse.

A stern trawler drags a large trawl net behind it. Ships like this were developed to catch huge shoals of cod at depths below 15m/50ft.

Fishing boats and nets

The type of net a boat carries depends on the fish it is going to catch. Some boats fish for species that live near the surface of the sea, while others trawl the waters deeper down. Floats and weights are attached to the net to keep it in shape under the water. For example, otter boards are used to force open the mouth of a trawl. There are regulations restricting the size of the holes in the net so that young fish can escape.

ANCHORS

A N ANCHOR is a device for stopping a ship or boat drifting in the wind or current. It is used when the engines are turned off or the sails taken down. The anchor is attached to the ship by a strong chain and its particular shape makes it embed firmly in the seabed. There are several reasons for using an anchor. The most common is for stopping close to shore when there is no harbour or the ship is too big for the harbour (such as an oil tanker). In an emergency, such as an engine failure in bad weather, an anchor can stop a ship drifting on to the shore and being wrecked. Different designs of anchor are suitable for different sizes of ships and for different types of seabed, such as sandy or rocky. The projects on these pages will show you how to make two different types of anchor that are used in very different conditions.

Ship's anchor
This type of anchor is called a stockless anchor and is used on most metal ships. The points of the anchor dig into the seabed, securing the ship.

MAKE A ROCK ANCHOR

You will need: *large paper clip, pliers, ruler, short pencil, rubber bands, thin garden cane, scissors, string, tray of pebbles (about 10cm/4in in size).*

Catching the rocks
Your model is similar to an anchor used on a traditional fishing boat. The spikes catch hold of the crevices on a rock-strewn seabed.

1 Unbend a large paper clip using pliers. Cut off 10cm/4in of wire and bend it slightly. Attach the wire to a short pencil with a rubber band wound tightly around the join.

2 Cut a piece of thin garden cane also 10cm/4in long. Attach this to the other end of the pencil, but at right angles to the wire. Use a rubber band to secure the cane.

3 Cut a long piece of string for an anchor chain. Tie one end of it to the pencil, below the garden cane. Fill a tray with pebbles to test out your anchor (see opposite).

MAKE A SAND ANCHOR

You will need: *large paper clips, pliers, sticky tape, plastic straw, scissors, sheet of plastic, coins, string, tray of sand.*

1 Bend a paper clip into a T-shape with a foot. Use pliers to cut another piece of wire to fit across the top of the T. Attach with tape and two lengths of plastic straw.

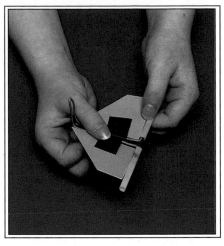

2 Cut two blades from a sheet of plastic. Make sure that they will fit inside your T-shape. Tape the blades securely to the upright of the T and the two straws.

blade

Digging into sand

This is a model of a Danforth anchor. The wide, flat blades dig deep into either a muddy or a sandy seabed.

3 Find two medium-size coins the same size. Tape one to each blade. The coins add weight to make it dig into the sand better.

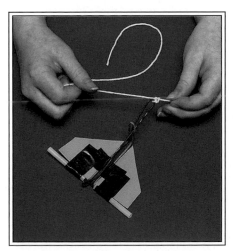

4 Shape another paper clip to make a straight arm with a hook at each end. Hook one end to the anchor and rest the arm in the upright foot. Tie a length of string to the other end. Use a tray of sand to test your anchor.

Testing your anchors

To test out your anchors, lay them on top of the sand or pebbles in the tray. Now pull the anchors along the length of the tray with the string. How well do they work? Try the anchors in the other trays. Do they still work as well now?

SAILING

SAILS CATCH the power of the wind to propel the boat or ship along. Today, sail power is mainly used by leisure craft, for racing and cruising. In some parts of the world, sail power is still common for fishing boats. Sails were originally made of strong cloth called canvas, but are now usually made of synthetic fabrics. Sails are supported by masts and ropes or wires called rigging. Ropes used to trim (adjust) sails are called sheets. Large yachts have different sets of sails for different wind conditions, including small storm sails. There are many different arrangements of masts, sails and rigging. Most modern sailboats and yachts have two triangular sails called a mainsail and jib supported by a single mast. The keel on a yacht and the centreboard on a sailboat stop the boat drifting sideways in the wind. A heavy keel also makes a yacht more stable.

mainsail — mainmast

batten (sail stiffener) — jib

boom

mainsheet

tiller

jibsheet — hull

rudder — centreboard

Parts of a sailboat
The main parts of a typical sailboat are shown above. A sailboat like this would usually have a crew of two people – a helmsman who operates the tiller and the mainsail and a crew who works the jib and centreboard. The jib is a small triangular sail in front of the mainmast. Sailboats also use spinnakers (three-cornered sails used in racing) for extra speed.

Racing sailboat
In very windy conditions, the helmsman and crew lean out over the side of the boat. They do this to keep the boat balanced and upright. The crew uses a harness called a trapeze attached to a wire running to the top of the mast. They lean out to the windward side of the boat.

Racing yacht
Large racing yachts have enormous sails and need a large crew to change them quickly. Sails are raised and lowered using winding wheels called winches. Yachts like this are designed to be sailed across oceans.

Cruising yacht

A cruising yacht has comfortable cabins, a galley and bathroom. It has smaller sails than a race yacht and is easier to sail. This type of yacht, rigged with one mast, is known as a sloop. It has two jib sails so it is called cutter rigged.

Fastest of all

The *Hydroptère* is the fastest sailing trimaran in the world. A trimaran has a main hull and two outriggers. The outriggers make the yacht very stable, which means it can use enormous sails for its size. Although multi-hulled vessels have been in use for centuries, offshore racing trimarans have been developed only since the 1960s.

Old designs

These big, two-masted yachts are called schooners. A schooner has a foremast ahead of the mainmast. Here, their sails are gaff rigged (supporting poles at an angle to the masts).

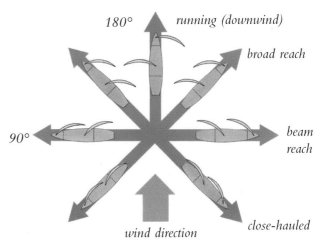

180° running (downwind)

broad reach

90°

beam reach

close-hauled

wind direction

Points of sailing

A boat can use the wind to sail in every direction, except straight into the wind. The crew adjust the sails to go in different directions called the points of sailing. To head upwind a boat must follow a zig-zag course. This is called tacking. If a boat turns when the wind is behind it, it is known as gybing. Running (sailing downwind) is not the fastest direction. Reaching (sailing across the wind) is faster.

FACT BOX

• The first person to sail solo around the world was Joshua Slocum from America. The voyage took three years and Slocum could not swim.

• The record time for sailing around the world is 45 days. It was set in 2012 by a yacht called *Bankque Populaire V*.

• In the galley (kitchen) of a yacht, the stove is mounted on hinges. This keeps it level when the boat heels over in the wind.

SAILS FOR POWER

THE PROJECT on these pages will show you how to make a model of a simple sailboat. Once you have made your model, use it to find out how a sailing boat works and how sailors use the wind. To sail in the direction the sailor wants to go, he or she must look at the direction that the wind is blowing from and adjust the position of the sails to make the most use of the wind. A boat can sail in every direction except straight into the wind. When a boat faces directly into the wind, its sails flap uselessly and the boat is in the no-go zone. To sail towards a place where the wind is blowing from, the sailors must sail a zig-zag course. This means first sailing across the wind one way, then sailing across it the other. This is called tacking. Making the most of the wind is the art of sailing and it takes lots of practice. Sailors have to learn to control many different parts of the boat at the same time.

Finished boat
Once you have finished your boat, you could try adding a centreboard. Does it make any difference to the boat's handling?

MAKE A SAILBOAT

You will need: *pencil, ruler, card (card stock), scissors, sticky tape, plastic sheet, stapler, bradawl (awl), non-hardening clay, thin garden canes, paper in various shades, plastic straws, small plastic bottle, string, paper clip.*

Template
Use this template for your model. The dimensions are 25x10cm/ 10x4in, with sides 4cm/1½in deep.

1 Cut out your hull shape from thick card, using the template above as a guide. Score along the broken lines with the scissors. Use sticky tape to attach the sides.

2 Lay the hull on a plastic sheet. Cut around it leaving a 5cm/2in gap around it to overlap the sides. Fold the plastic over the sides of the hull and staple it in place.

3 Pierce a hole in a strip of card a little wider than the hull. Staple in place. Put some clay under the hole. Push a 30cm/1ft cane through into the clay.

4 Cut a sail from paper. Attach a straw along the side and a cane along the bottom with sticky tape. Slip the straw over the mast.

5 Cut an L-shape (about 8cm/3in long, 4cm/1½in wide at base and 2cm/¾in wide at top) from the small plastic bottle. Cut the base of the L in half to make two tabs, as shown.

6 Fold back the L-shape's two tabs in opposite directions and staple them to the stern (back) of the boat. This is the boat's rudder.

Finding out about the points of sailing

When you test your boat out, try setting the sails in these different positions. Alter the position of the sail by using the string taped to the boom (cane). Follow the arrows shown here to see which way the wind should be blowing from in each case. Why not try blowing from other directions to see if this makes a difference to your boat?

direction of wind

8 To test out how your sail boat works, make a breeze by waving a large sheet of paper near to the boat. Adjust the string to move the sail in to the right position.

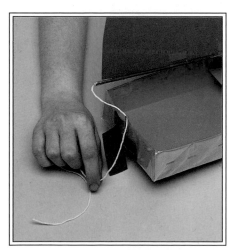

7 Cut a piece of string about 20cm/8in long. Tape one end to the back of the boom (the cane) and feed the other end through a paper clip attached to the back of the boat.

WARSHIPS

THE FIRST true warships were the many-oared galleys of ancient Greece and Rome. By the 1400s, heavily-armed galleons with many cannons were developed. In the early 1900s, steam-driven, iron battleships were the forerunners of modern warships. Today's warships carry a huge amount of special equipment. They have weapons for attacking other ships and submarines, weapons for defending themselves against air attack, and electronic equipment for tracking ships and aircraft and controlling their weapons. The largest warships are aircraft carriers, which act as air bases at sea. Smaller warships, such as frigates and destroyers, are designed for speed and have powerful gas turbine engines. The smallest ships are minesweepers and patrol boats. A country's navy defends its waters, transports and supports fighting troops and helps in emergencies around the world. A navy needs many ships to keep its warships supplied with fuel, food and ammunition.

Operations room
At the heart of a warship is the operations room. From here the crew monitor what other ships and aircraft are doing and make decisions about what actions to take.

Destroyer
A destroyer is generally larger than a frigate and is an all-purpose warship. This guided-missile destroyer has several radar dishes for weapons control as well as navigation. It also has a helicopter deck at the stern.

FACT BOX
• Aircraft carriers are the largest warships. They have displacements of more than 90,000 tons and crews of 5,000 sailors and air crew.

• During World War I (1914–18) battleships with huge guns fought at sea. Hulls were protected by 40cm/16in thick armour.

• The largest submarines are Russian Typhoon class. They have displacements of 24,400 tons and are 175m/574ft long.

Frigate
A frigate is a small, fast-moving ship used to escort convoys of larger ships. It carries anti-submarine and anti-aircraft weapons. Small frigates are sometimes called corvettes.

helicopter deck

anti-aircraft missile launcher

radars and communication aerials (antenna)

funnel

rocket launcher

gun turret

bridge

anti-aircraft missile launcher

Exocet missile launcher

Parts of a warship
This is an overhead view of a frigate. You can clearly see the sharp bows and narrow hull that help to give it speed. It has a range of guns and missiles aboard ship as well as armed helicopters.

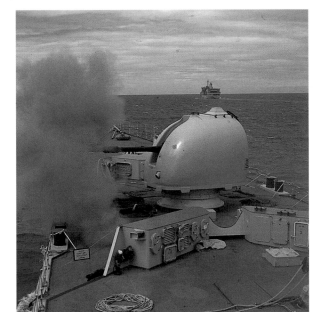

Naval guns
Modern naval guns, such as this 114mm single gun, are aimed automatically. A fire-control radar keeps track of the target and moves the gun from side to side and up and down. Missiles are also used to bring down enemy aircraft. Some have on-board sensors that home in on their target.

Airfield at sea
An aircraft carrier's deck is a runway where aircraft take off and land. The runway is short so a steam catapult is used to help launch the aircraft at take-off. Underneath the deck is a hangar where aircraft are stored and serviced. The aircrafts' wings fold up to save storage space below deck.

Support ships
This ship is a specialized support ship used in landing troops. In the stern is a dock for landing craft to be loaded. The landing craft are used to ferry troops and equipment to the shore.

Inflatables
Special forces, such as commandos, use small, fast inflatable craft for transferring from ship to shore. This boat can be used above the water or underwater as a diving craft. It can even be submerged and hidden on the seabed until it is needed. You can see the electrically powered propeller for underwater use.

inflatable dinghy (small boat) is powered by two outboard motors

SUBMARINES

*view
of outside*

*view
of inside*

A SUBMARINE is a vessel that can travel submerged under the water as well as on the water's surface. Most submarines are naval ships. There are two main types – hunter-killer, or patrol submarines, which search for and try to sink enemy shipping, and ballistic missile submarines, which carry nuclear missiles. Naval submarines use two different types of power – conventional and nuclear. When a conventional submarine is on the surface its diesel engine makes electricity. The electricity is used to run the electric motors that work the propeller and also to recharge the batteries. When the submarine is submerged, the diesel engine is turned off and the electric motor is powered by the batteries. In a nuclear submarine, the power comes from a nuclear reactor. The main weapon of a hunter-killer submarine is the torpedo – a sort of underwater missile. Another type of underwater vessel is the submersible. Submersibles are small diving craft used for ocean research, exploration and the repair of undersea pipes and cables.

The *Turtle*

American engineer David Bushnell built the first working submarine in 1775. It was called the *Turtle* and made of wood. It was moved by two screw-shaped, hand-operated propellers.

Nuclear submarine

A nuclear submarine, such as this Trident, can stay submerged for months on end. Its reactor can run for this long without refuelling.

An air conditioning plant recycles the air on board to make fresh air.

U-boat

The potential of the submarine as a weapon was realized during World War II (1939–45). The German U-boats (*Unterseeboot*) had greatly increased range and speed. They sank thousands of Allied ships with their torpedoes.

Parts of a submarine

A modern submarine, such as this nuclear ballistic missile submarine, is around 91m/ 100 yards long. It has a crew of around 140 who work in shifts. Like other ships, it has an engine, propeller and rudder at the stern. Heat from the nuclear reactor generates steam. This drives the turbines that turn the submarine's propeller. Like all submarines, its hull is strong, but very few submarines can go below 500m/1,640ft. Buoyancy tanks fill with water to submerge the submarine. To resurface, compressed air pushes the water out of the tanks. Small movable wings, called hydroplanes, control the submarine's direction.

Towers and periscopes

The conning tower stands clear of the water when a submarine surfaces. Communication masts and periscopes top the tower. A periscopes is a device that allows the crew to see above water when the submarine is submerged. There are usually two periscopes – a large one for general observation and a smaller one for attack.

stabilizer fin   *turbine*   *communication antenna*   *periscope*   *torpedo room*   *torpedo tube*

conning tower

aft hydroplane   *electric motor*   *nuclear reactor*   *missile tube*   *control room*   *crew's living quarters*   *forward hydroplane*   *sonar array*

Mini-submersible

Small submersibles, carrying one or two people, are used to work at depths that would be too dangerous for a free-swimming diver. They are equipped with cameras, floodlights and robot arms. Highly accurate navigation systems allow the crew to find their way in the pitch black of the seabed. A mini-submersible runs on batteries and can stay under for only a short time – less than a day.

Research submersible

Teams of people dive to the ocean floor in submersibles. They have extremely strong hulls for diving very deep, up to 8km/5 miles. They dive and return to a support ship waiting on the surface. Special, deep-diving vessels called bathyscaphes can dive even farther – up to 11km/7 miles.

DIVING AND SURFACING

tanks are full of air and valves are closed

valves open and tanks fill with water

tanks full, submarine submerged

air is forced in, so water is forced out

A submarine dives by making itself heavier so that it sinks. It surfaces again by making itself lighter. To do this, it uses large tanks called buoyancy tanks. When the submarine is on the surface, the buoyancy tanks are full of air. To make the submarine dive, the tanks are flooded with seawater, making the submarine heavy enough to sink. To make the submarine surface again, compressed air is pumped into the tanks, forcing the water out. This makes the submarine lighter and it floats to the surface. In this project, you can make a model submarine that can dive and surface using buoyancy tanks. When it is underwater, a full-scale submarine moves up and down using hydroplanes. These are like tiny wings and work like rudders as the submarine moves along. Submarines need very strong hulls to prevent them from being crushed by the huge pressure under the water. As submarines dive down, the weight of the water pressing down on them becomes greater and greater. The tremendous pressure from the water builds up quickly.

MAKE A SUBMARINE

***You will need:** large plastic bottle, sand, plastic funnel, two small plastic bottles, bradawl (awl), scissors, ruler, two plastic drinking straws, rubber bands, non-hardening clay, two small bulldog clips.*

Diving and surfacing

Water is let into buoyancy tanks by opening valves to let the air out. Water is expelled by pumping in air stored in tanks of compressed air.

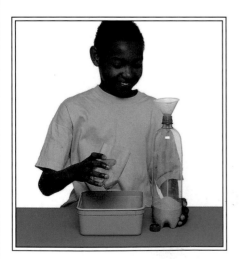

1 Fill the large plastic bottle with sand using a funnel. Fill it until it just sinks in a tank of water. Test out the bottle (cap firmly screwed on) to find the right amount of sand.

2 Make a large hole (about 1cm/ ½in across) in one side of two small plastic bottles. On the other side make a small hole, big enough for a plastic straw to fit into.

3 Attach the two small bottles to either side of the large bottle using rubber bands. Twist the small bottles so that the small hole on each one points upwards.

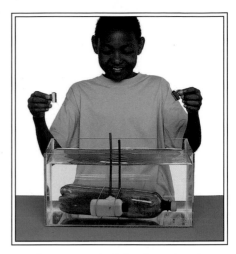

4 Push a plastic drinking straw into each small hole so that a bit pokes through. Seal the base of the straws with clay to make a watertight join.

5 Put a small bulldog clip about halfway down each straw. The clips need to be strong enough to squash the straw and stop air being forced out by the water.

6 Put your model submarine in a tank of water. With the clips on it should float. Remove the clips and water will flood the buoyancy tanks. The submarine will sink.

Final adjustments
This is the finished model submarine. You might find your model sinks bow first, or stern first. If this is the case, level it by shaking the sand evenly inside the bottle.

8 When your model submarine has resurfaced, keep blowing slowly into the tanks. Replace each bulldog clip and your model submarine will remain floating on the surface.

7 To make the submarine surface again, blow slowly into both straws at once. The air will force the water out of the buoyancy tanks and the submarine will rise to the surface.

PLEASURE CRAFT

Wind and waves
In strong winds a windsurfer can perform amazing flying leaps using a funboard. The surfboard is steered by a sail. Experienced surfers take part in competitions, such as course racing and wave performance.

T HERE ARE many boats and ships designed for relaxation and sport. Boats offer a huge range of activities, from hiring a rowboat to cruising the oceans in a luxury yacht. Many people enjoy cruising and touring vacations afloat. Some people operate the boat themselves, while others prefer to relax and have a crew to do the sailing. The ocean liners that regularly sailed across the world's seas have long gone, but their place has been taken by cruise liners. These ships are like floating hotels and are specifically designed for tourists. A cruise ship usually calls at a number of ports. Some enthusiasts even sail all the way around the world. Watersports such as rowing, canoeing, sailing and windsurfing are popular. Spectacular tricks and stunts can be executed on windsurfers, surfboards and body boards. Canoes and kayaks offer the excitement of shooting down white-water rapids. Other people enjoy racing in sailboats, yachts, rowing boats and powerboats, and on jetskis.

White-water racing
A kayak has a closed cockpit so that no water can get into the hull, even in very rough water. This makes it excellent for white-water racing. There are two types of racing. In wildwater racing, canoeists are timed over a course of obstacles such as rocks and rapids. In slalom, canoeists negotiate a course of gates.

Touring canoe
The canoe is an open boat, as opposed to the closed cockpit of a kayak. The canoeist sits or kneels and can use either single or double-bladed paddles. Canadian canoes are used for slalom races over a set course. Open canoes are a good way of seeing the natural world, because they move quietly through the water, not disturbing the peace.

Rafting

Heading down the turbulent waters of a mountain river in an inflatable raft is a popular adventure sport. Rafters use single-bladed paddles. Everybody wears a lifejacket because there is a danger of falling out of the raft.

Sailing cruiser

Many people enjoy days out and longer trips on sailing cruisers. This yacht, the *Wind Spirit*, is a cross between a sailing yacht and a cruise liner.

Luxury cruiser

A few people are lucky enough to be able to afford a large luxury motor yacht, or cruiser, like this. These yachts are equipped with every sort of luxury as well as the latest in satellite navigation equipment and cruise control.

Powerboat racing

A ride in a powerboat is incredibly fast, but very bumpy. Their hulls are specially shaped to skim across the surface. There are two types of powerboat racing – inshore and offshore. Boats are put into different classes, depending on their size and engine. Fast Formula 1 powerboats race all over the world.

Cruise liner

Many people like to take trips on cruise liners. The liners travel around the world, stopping at interesting ports. A large cruise liner is part resort and part luxury hotel. It may be equipped with sundecks, swimming pool, whirlpool, tennis courts, gym, theatre and even a golf course.

SERVICE BOATS

SERVICE VESSELS do special jobs in rivers or at sea to help other boats and ships. The most common service boat is the tug. The tug's main job is to move other ships, sometimes to tow them into port, other times because their engines have failed. The largest tugs, called salvage tugs, can tow even huge cargo ships and also help in emergency situations. Tugs have high bows to break through large waves, a high bridge to give a good view, a large deck to carry cargo and on-board winches. They also have extremely powerful engines and are highly manoeuvrable. A selection of service vessels is shown here. There are many more, however, such as cable-laying ships, oil drilling vessels and light ships. Lifeboats are also service boats.

Towing to sea
These tugs are towing part of an oil rig. They will tow it all the way from where is was built to its station at sea. Each tug has a strong towing hook where two steel ropes are attached.

Dredger
A dredger digs silt (mud and particles carried by water) from the bottom of rivers and canals. It does this to stop them becoming too shallow. A bucket dredger is shown below. It uses a long line of buckets to scoop silt into a barge.

Research ship
An ocean research ship is a floating science laboratory. This ship has a bathymetry system for surveying the seabed. It also has on-board computer systems and equipment for lowering instruments and submersibles into the sea. It can carry 18 marine and technical staff on voyages of over 40 days. The engines have been specially modified to reduce engine noise, which might affect sensitive recordings. Research vessels like this help biologists to explore life on the seabed. They also help oceanographers (scientists who study the oceans) to examine undersea mountains and trenches.

two tugs manoeuvre the bow

supertanker

two tugs push the stern

the tugs push on opposite sides to turn the ship around

Pushing around

These tugs are manoeuvring a huge supertanker into port. The tanker is so big it has difficulty steering in enclosed waters. Tugs using towlines and pushing with their bows can turn the ship around. They gently nudge it into its berth or to an offshore mooring buoy.

Fire fighting

Every major port has a fire-fighting tug on stand-by all the time. It sprays foam or water, which is sucked from the sea by powerful pumps. The water is fired from guns on the upper deck on to burning ships or port buildings. Foam is used to smother oil and chemical fires from tankers.

Floating crane

A salvage barge is like a floating crane. It is used to recover sunken or capsized vessels. Huge cranes like this can lift large cargo ships from the seabed.

Breaking the ice

An icebreaker has a very strong hull. It is designed to ride up on the ice so that the ship's weight breaks through the thick ice. Most icebreakers have propellers in the bow to draw the smashed ice back behind the ship. Some also have special tanks on board to allow the ship to heel over if necessary to free it from the surrounding ice. Icebreakers are used to keep shipping lanes in northern waters open during winter. They are used in countries such as Canada, Denmark, Russia, Sweden and the United States.

NAVIGATION AND SIGNALS

one

two

three

AT SEA, navigation includes many different jobs. It involves planning a safe route, checking the ship's position regularly to see how it is progressing, avoiding collisions with other vessels, and keeping an eye on the weather. The basic tools of navigation are a chart (map) of the sea and a magnetic compass. The chart shows coastlines, the depth of the water, landmarks on shore, hazards such as wrecks, the strength of tides and so on. Modern navigating tools, such as satellite-controlled Global Positioning System (GPS), mean that boats and ships with the correct equipment always know their position. Lighthouses and buoys help with navigation by indicating safe shipping channels and hazards. Signals are a way of sending messages to the shore or another vessel without using radio. Ways to signal include signal flags and lamps.

Signal flags

An international system of signal flags has been used for centuries. Each flag stands for a number, a letter or a complete message. A flag's basic meaning can be changed by hoisting it on a different mast or in a certain combination with other flags. A selection of flags, with their meanings, is shown here.

C (yes)

N (no)

A light at sea

A lighthouse warns of dangerous islands, rocks and headlands. It sends out a bright beam of light that sweeps around in a circle. At sea, it appears as a flashing light. Anchored light ships are also used to mark treacherous spots.

O (man overboard)

Signal lamp

Morse code (a code of long and short pulses) is another way of sending messages. An Aldis lamp has a trigger that the operator uses to turn the light on and off.

Aldis lamp

G (I require a pilot)

lantern

When lighthouses needed people to run them, the crew's quarters were in the tower. Today, most are on automatic.

compass rose

nautical charts

dividers

magnetic compass

Navigation tools

The simple equipment here can be used to plot a course on a chart. Plotting a course involves drawing a series of lines on the chart that the ship will follow. The pilot also checks the boat's position from landmarks. Shown on the chart is the compass rose used for taking bearings (directions).

parallel ruler

marine GPS system

A red port buoy marks the lefthand side of a channel.

A green starboard buoy marks the righthand side of a channel.

Yellow and black cardinal buoys mark hazards or points of interest.

Navigation buoys

The shape and colour of a buoy give it its meaning. Most buoys are red or green and indicate the sides of a safe channel. All buoys have flashing lights as well.

Electronic navigation

The navigation equipment on a modern ship includes radar, sonar and satellite receivers. Radar shows the position of the coast and other ships. Sonar shows the depth of water under the ship. Satellite GPS gives the ship's exact position to within a few metres.

Computers in navigation

At the chart table of this yacht are several computers. One receives images directly from a weather satellite. Another displays the ship's position on an electronic chart.

NAVIGATION LIGHTS

Moving to starboard (right).

THERE are no street lights at sea, so all vessels have to display lights to warn other vessels that they are there. The types of light and number of them depend on the size of the vessel and what it is doing. For example, a sailboat must carry a white light at the top of its mast. A small powered boat that is underway must carry a red/green light and a white light above it. A red light is always hung on the port side (the lefthand side as you face the bow) of a boat or ship, while a green light is hung on the starboard (right). The project on these pages will show you how to make a simple red/green light. Larger ships that are underway carry a red/green light and several white lights. From these lights, the crew of one ship can tell what size another ship is, whether it is moving and which direction it is going in. This is especially important at night or in fog when visibility is poor. Fishing boats also display extra coloured lights when they are fishing so that other ships can avoid their nets.

Moving to port (left).

Heading straight ahead.

MAKE A NAVIGATION LIGHT

You will need: *pencil, ruler, thick card, scissors, four insulated wires, screwdriver, two bulb holders and bulbs, non-hardening clay, sticky tape, clear plastic bottle, red and green plastic, battery.*

Which way?
The shade of light you can see (red, green or both) shows which way the ship is moving.

1 Draw out a simple boat shape about 30cm/12in long and 20cm/8in wide on a sheet of thick card. Give the shape a pointed bow and a flat stern. Cut out your shape.

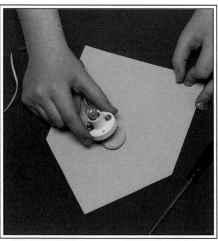

2 Attach two wires to a bulb holder, one either side. Screw in a bulb. Fix the holder to the middle of your boat shape with a piece of non-hardening clay.

3 Cut three rectangles of card, about 10x6cm/4x2½in. Trim one corner of each piece to fit around the bulb and holder. When secure they will divide up the light.

4 Fix the trimmed ends of the three pieces of card together. Fit over the bulb and stick to the boat base.

5 Cut two rectangles of plastic from a bottle. Tape green transparent plastic to one and red to the other.

6 Tape the red plastic to the left (port) side of the boat. Tape the green to the right (starboard) side.

7 Cut a circle of card and tape it over the bulb and tinted windows to make a lid. Fix another bulb and bulb holder with wires attached to the top of the boat.

8 Now attach a battery. Tape a wire from each bulb to one end of the battery. Tape the other two wires to the other end of the battery. Both bulbs should light up.

9 Try testing out your red/green light in a darkened room. Ask a friend to observe while you walk towards him or her. Can they tell which way the boat is moving? Is it coming towards him, away from him, to his left, or to his right?

SHIPPING DISASTERS

THE SEAS and oceans can be very dangerous places. Every year, hundreds of ships are lost and many of their crews drown. The worst hazard is the weather. Strong winds blowing across a wide expanse of water create huge waves as tall as a house. The waves can swamp a small boat or cause a ship to capsize. Long, high waves can break the back of a ship if they lift its bow and stern, leaving its centre unsupported. Another main cause of accidents is human error. Mistakes in communication or navigation cause collisions between vessels, perhaps sinking one of them. Ships also run aground through errors in navigation. Other accidents are caused by engine failures, fires or explosions. These can have very serious consequences if a ship is carrying a dangerous cargo that may cause long-lasting damage to the environment.

Running aground
Once a ship has run aground it is hard to refloat. If it runs aground on rocks it may even be holed. Eventually a wreck like this will break up in the waves.

Fire on board
Despite being surrounded by water, fire is one of the worst hazards at sea. This ship is lucky that there is a fire boat in range. Usually the crew have to fight the fire themselves.

FACT BOX
• At sea, distances are measured in nautical miles. One nautical mile equals 1,852m/6,076ft. Speed is measured in knots – nautical miles per hour.

• Depth was once measured in fathoms. One fathom was 6ft, which equals 1.83m.

• The biggest collision at sea was between two oil tankers. Their combined deadweight was 660,000 tonnes. Around 300,000 tonnes of oil were spilt into the Caribbean Sea.

Tanker disaster
The oil tanker *MV Braer* ran aground in the Shetland Islands, Scotland, in 1993. The hull was holed and 80,000 tonnes of oil leaked into the sea, creating a huge oil slick. Spills like this result in major ecological damage.

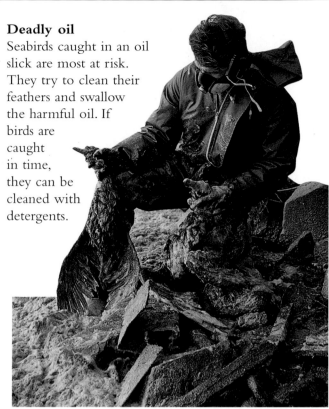

Deadly oil
Seabirds caught in an oil slick are most at risk. They try to clean their feathers and swallow the harmful oil. If birds are caught in time, they can be cleaned with detergents.

Beach clean up
If an oil slick reaches the shore, it coats the rocks with oily sludge. Clearing up a large spill with suction pumps takes months and is very expensive. The coastline takes years to recover.

Capsize
The *Costa Concordia*, a large cruise ship, struck rocks in shallow water off Italy's west coast and partially sank on January 13, 2012, claiming 32 lives. After the grounding, most of passengers and crew were rescued by lifeboats and helicopters or swam to the nearby island.

The sinking of the *Titanic*
The most famous shipping disaster of all was the sinking of the ocean liner *Titanic* on April 15, 1912. With the loss of 1,517 lives, it remains one of the worst peacetime disasters. This painting of the event is exaggerated – the ship's hull was holed by ice under the water. The disaster was made worse because there were not enough lifeboats.

IN AN EMERGENCY

Lifeboat stations
In an emergency, passengers on this cruise liner would get in the lifeboats shown here. The lifeboats would be lowered down the side of the ship, into the sea.

W HEN AN ACCIDENT does happen, the crew immediately begin to follow an emergency procedure. If they have a radio, they will send a May Day call to the emergency services. Other vessels in the area will go to help, a lifeboat may be launched, or a helicopter sent to search. To help rescuers locate their stricken vessel, flares are fired and emergency horns sounded. Larger boats and ships have an automatic radio beacon that sends out a distress call when it falls into the sea. The emergency services can home in on the beacon. If the crew have to abandon ship, they put on life jackets, perhaps survival suits, and launch lifeboats or life rafts. All but the smallest vessels have fire-fighting equipment on board. A cruise liner will have a computerized warning and sprinkler system.

FACT BOX
• Ships on which there is a risk of explosion, such as drilling and gas-carrying ships, have lifeboats next to the crew compartments. These drop into the sea for quick evacuation.

• If a submarine cannot surface, its crew escape in buoyant personal escape suits. These act as life rafts on the surface.

• The crew of an offshore lifeboat wear helmets and are harnessed to their seats to stop them flying about as waves crash into the boat.

Inshore lifeboats
Small lifeboats, such as this Australian surfboat, help to rescue people near the coast. Swimmers, surfers and sailboat users are rescued quickly by boats like this. It is specially designed to ride over the high surf.

Lifeboat launch
Offshore lifeboats can be swiftly launched down a slipway. When the emergency call comes through, the crew jump into the boat, start the engine and release a holding wire. The boat hits the water at speed. This is a much faster way to launch a boat than setting off from a harbour.

Life rafts

Inflatable life rafts are stored in a container on the deck of a ship or yacht. When the container is thrown into the sea, the raft inflates automatically. It is designed to maintain body heat and not capsize. Inside the raft are medical and food supplies.

Lifeboat at sea

Offshore lifeboats are designed to operate in the worst weather at sea. They have very powerful engines for reaching an emergency quickly. Lifeboats are self-righting and quickly come upright if a wave knocks them flat.

Helicopter rescue

A Search and Rescue helicopter winchman is lowered to pick up a casualty. Air-sea rescue helicopters take part in searches, winch crew from stricken ships and carry casualties quickly to hospitals on shore.

foghorn

flares

The coastguard

Some countries have coastal patrol boats. This Canadian patrol boat is operated by the coastguard service. It acts as a police boat as well as a lifeboat.

Flares and horns

Sailors in trouble fire flares and sound foghorns to show up their position. Flares are like large fireworks. Some simply burn brightly. Others fire a burning light into the sky. The foghorn uses compressed air to make an ear-piercing noise.

KEEPING AFLOAT

MAKE A SELF-RIGHTING BOAT

You will need: pencil, ruler, polystyrene (styrofoam) tile, scissors, non-hardening clay, rubber bands, small plastic tub.

A CREW'S first reaction in a collision or grounding is to try to keep their ship afloat if possible. For a start, all ships have bilge pumps. These are used to pump water out of the bottom of the boat's hull and into the sea. Small boats, such as sailboats and canoes, have bags of air or blocks of polystyrene inside to keep them afloat. Most lifeboats are self-righting, which means that they bob back upright if they capsize. Lifeboats are built of tough, lightweight materials such as plastic and foam. They are completely watertight – even their air inlets have seals to keep out the water. Their heavy engines are set low down, while the hull and high-up cabins are full of air. This arrangement ensures that the lifeboat flips upright without needing help. You can find out how to make a simple self-righting boat in the first project.

The hull of a large ship below the waterline is divided into watertight sections by strong metal walls called bulkheads. The doors in the bulkheads are also watertight when they are closed. These are designed so that if one section floods, the water cannot fill the whole hull. Even if a ship is sinking, bulkheads stop it from capsizing due to water rushing to one side. In the second project you can test out how a hull with bulkheads works much better than one without bulkheads.

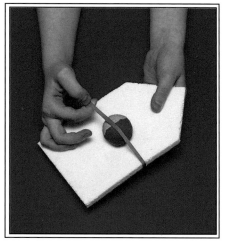

1 Cut a boat shape 15x10cm/ 6x4in from polystyrene. Attach a golf-ball size lump of clay to one side with a rubber band.

2 Put your boat into a tank or bowl of water. Have the clay, which represents the crew and equipment, on top. If you capsize the boat it will stay capsized.

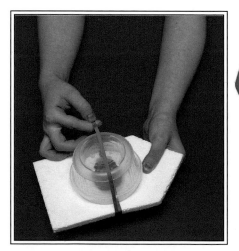

3 Add another lump of clay underneath the boat to represent heavy engines or ballast. Add an upturned plastic tub on top to represent a watertight cabin.

4 Now try to capsize it again and it will flip back upright. This is because air trapped underwater by the tub and a heavy weight on top forces the boat upright again.

INSTALLING BULKHEADS

You will need: *plastic container and lid, bradawl (awl), marbles, scissors, non-hardening clay, wooden blocks.*

1 Pierce a hole in one corner of a plastic container using a bradawl. This represents the holed hull of a cargo ship.

2 Add some marbles (cargo) and lower the container into a tank of water. It will fill up with water and slowly sink.

3 Cut three rectangles from the lid of the container. Make sure they fit across the tub. Round off the bottom corners if you need to.

5 Put some cargo in each section of the hull and put the whole thing back into the water. This time the container will stay afloat because only one section floods. The bulkheads prevent the water filling the whole hull.

Sinking feeling
Find out how many sections need to be holed before the container will sink.

4 Position the plastic walls inside the container so that they divide it into four compartments. Press clay around the edges to make a watertight seal.

IN PORT

SHIPS AND BOATS move cargo and people from place to place, so they need ports where they can load and unload. Every port has areas called docks where ships tie up along the quayside. The docks are often inside an area of water called a harbour, which is protected from the sea by a massive stone wall or natural cliffs. On the dock are huge cranes for unloading the ships and warehouses for storing cargo. In the port area there may be ship repair yards, parts shops and customs offices. Until recently, large numbers of people were employed as dockers and many major coastal towns and cities have grown up around ports. But the increased use of containers has dramatically reduced the number of workers. Huge merchant ships now dock at purpose-built ports or terminals, which are specially designed for handling cargoes, such as containers, oil and gas.

Tying up
Berthing ropes hooked over bollards are used to tie ships to the quayside. Quays may also be known as wharves.

Container port
An aerial view shows part of Hong Kong's vast container terminal. Special loading cranes, called straddle carriers, are used to fetch and carry the containers.

The pilot
The entrance to a harbour is often narrow and busy. It may also have treacherous shallow areas such as sandbanks outside it. A pilot is a person who knows the harbour well. He or she always takes control of large ships to guide them as they enter and leave the port.

Unloading in port

A dockside crane unloads a Japanese ship in the port of Vladivostock, Russia. The crane can be moved along the dockside on railway tracks. This ship's decks, as well as its hold, are piled with freight packed in boxes called tea chests.

Old harbours

The old harbour at Sydney, Australia, is a popular tourist attraction. Many old docks are too small for modern merchant ships. After years of neglect, their harbours are being renovated to provide leisure facilities.

High and dry

Repair and maintenance facilities in port may include a dry dock. This submarine is being repaired in dry dock. The submarine entered the dock when it was flooded with water. The gates were then closed and the water pumped out. Scaffolding is erected to keep the submarine upright.

Marina

A marina is a small harbour area where leisure craft, such as motorboats and sailing yachts, tie up. Marinas are usually separate from the normal harbour. They are also common on coasts where there are few natural harbours for small boats to shelter in. Each bay, called a berth, in a marina has water and electricity supplies.

INDEX